M000013183

A
Baby's World

Compiled by
Lisa Berman

Design by Michel Design

P PETER PAUPER PRESS, INC.
WHITE PLAINS · NEW YORK

Copyright © 1992
Peter Pauper Press, Inc.
202 Mamaroneck Avenue
White Plains, NY 10601
All rights reserved
ISBN 0-88088-755-9
Printed in Hong Kong
7 6 5 4 3 2

A BABY'S WORLD

Children are a kind of confirmation of life. The only form of immortality that we can be sure of.

Peter Ustinov

I've always felt I've had luck, certainly in the obvious areas. And now I have the greatest blessing of all—these children.

Jessica Lange

*H*ow to fold a diaper depends on the size of the baby and the diaper.

Dr. Benjamin Spock,
Baby and Child Care

*G*ARY: I just don't understand. I mean, women have been having babies for thousands of years and you'd think it would have gotten easier . . .

thirtysomething

CHESTER: My God, the human baby! A few weeks after birth, any other animal can fend for itself. But *you!* A basket case till you're twenty-one.

Megan Terry,
The Magic Realist

Children are life renewing itself, Captain Butler. And when life does that, danger seems very unimportant.

Olivia de Havilland,
in Gone With The Wind

A family can bring up a
baby only by being brought
up by him.

Erik Erikson

*E*very child is born a genius.

R. Buckminster Fuller

KATH: Can he be present at the birth of his child? . . .
ED: It's all any reasonable child can expect if the dad is present at the conception.

Joe Orton,
Entertaining Mr. Sloane

I often think it's comical
How Nature does contrive
That every boy and every gal,
That's born into the world
    alive,
Is either a little Liberal,
Or else a little Conservative!

W. S. Gilbert,
Iolanthe

*M*y mother groan'd,
my father wept,
Into the dangerous world
I leapt.

William Blake

The pains of childbirth
were altogether different
from the enveloping effects
of other kinds of pain. These
were pains one could follow
with one's mind.

Margaret Mead

*C*hildren reinvent your world for you. They're thrown into the works just to make sure you're not getting too stagnant.

Susan Sarandon

*I*f new-borns could
remember and speak, they
would emerge from the
womb carrying tales as
wondrous as Homer's.

Newsweek

*I*n healthy development the infant (theoretically) starts off (psychologically) without life and becomes lively simply because of being, in fact, alive.

D. W. Winnicott

*W*ell, Vashti, all you can do is raise them. You can't live their lives for them.

Elizabeth Taylor,
Giant

All my life I've been tremendously lonely. Having a child was a salve to my loneliness. You have these relationships with men, are in love and loved, but there's nothing like the need of a child.

Jessica Lange

*T*he sweetest flowers in all
the world—
A baby's hands.

Swinburne

Where did you come from,
 baby dear?
Out of the everywhere
 into here.

George MacDonald

*P*arents are people who
bear children, bore teenagers,
and board newlyweds.

Anonymous

*T*he period following
birth must be regarded as the
time when the nourishment
given to a child has the
greatest effect on the development of the body.

Aristotle

*W*ith children, you don't have any reason not to trust them, because they'll truly tell you like it is. They'll say "I love you," they'll say "Don't touch me," they'll say "I don't want you." You always know where you stand.

Demi Moore

O child! O new-born
  denizen
Of life's great city! on
  thy head
The glory of the morn
  is shed,
Like a celestial benison!

Longfellow

*D*on't be afraid to kiss
your baby when you feel like
it.

Dr. Benjamin Spock

*L*ove your children with all your hearts, love them enough to discipline them before it is too late. . . . Praise them for important things, even if you have to stretch them a bit. Praise them a lot. They live on it like bread and butter and they need it more than bread and butter.

Lavina Christensen Fugal

*T*hough parents have a dozen children, each is the only one.

Leo Rosten

*Y*ou don't want to leave home in the morning and you can't wait to get home at night. She's a year-and-a-half and she's changing all the time.

John Goodman,
on the impact of fatherhood

$\mathcal{P}$retty much all the honest truth telling there is in the world is done by children.

Oliver Wendell Holmes

*Y*ou were once a new baby. You had a special place in your family then—and you still have a special place in your family now. You always will—no matter how many children your mom and dad have.

Mr. Rogers

*A*llow children to be happy in their own way, for what better way will they ever find?

Samuel Johnson

The right moment to begin the requisite moral training is the moment of birth, because then it can be begun without disappointing expectations.

Bertrand Russell

We can't form our children on our own concepts; we must take them and love them as God gives them to us.

Goethe

*I*t is easier to have
children than raise them.

Leo Rosten

_M_ y mother dandled
me and sang, "How young it
is, how young!"

William Butler Yeats

H ush-a-bye baby, on
the tree top,
When the wind blows the
cradle will rock;
When the bough breaks the
cradle will fall,
Down will come baby,
cradle, and all.

Mother Goose

*T*his is the reason why mothers are more devoted to their children than fathers: it is that they suffer more in giving them birth and are more certain that they are their own.

Aristotle

*C*hildren in a family are
like flowers in a bouquet:
there's always one determined
to face in an opposite
direction from the way the
arranger desires.

Marcelene Cox

*E*very child is an artist.
The problem is how to
remain an artist once he
grows up.

Pablo Picasso

The thing you learn about children is that they are people in their own right, and you can't really do an awful lot with them. You can't change them.

Mick Jagger

We find delight in the beauty and happiness of children that makes the heart too big for the body.

Ralph Waldo Emerson

*D*o you remember that scene in *The World According to Garp* when he said, "Let's just sit here and watch the kids?" We do that. We sit here and watch them play. And it's, like, the greatest thing in the world.

Melanie Griffith

*W*hen the first baby laughed for the first time, the laugh broke into a thousand pieces and they all went skipping about, and that was the beginning of fairies.

James M. Barrie,
Peter Pan

A man finds out what is meant by a spitting image when he tries to feed cereal to his infant.

Imogene Fey

*A*s my fathers planted
for me, so do I plant for my
children.

Talmud

There would be no way, in my sane mind, that I wouldn't regret having married Carl [Bernstein], except for the children, who are so cosmically wonderful that I'm thrilled I married Carl.

Nora Ephron

*C*hildren need models
rather than critics.

Joseph Joubert

*S*he's more fun to watch
than an ant farm.

John Goodman,
about his daughter

*T*here is no finer invest-
ment for any community
than putting milk into babies.

Winston Churchill

I have a feeling Warren Beatty is having a baby so he can meet babysitters.

David Letterman

There are times I feel so close to the edge I could easily tip over. Then, other times, I feel much more centered. If it weren't for the kids, I could very well be gone, emotionally or physically. These kids have been my salvation.

Jessica Lange

All human beings are
born free and equal in
dignity and rights.

*Universal Declaration
of Human Rights*

*T*oo often we give children
answers to remember rather
than problems to solve.

Roger Lewin

Women's Liberation is just a lot of foolishness. It's the men who are discriminated against. They can't bear children. And no one's likely to do anything about that.

Golda Meir

A nything which parents
have not learned from
experience they can now
learn from their children.

Anonymous

*I*f a child is to keep alive
his inborn sense of wonder
without any such gift from
the fairies, he needs the
companionship of at least
one adult who can share it,
rediscovering with him the
joy, excitement and mystery
of the world we live in.

Rachel Carson

*F*ather asked us what was God's noblest work. Anna said *men*, but I said *babies*. Men are often bad; babies never are.

Louisa May Alcott

To talk to a child, to fascinate him, is much more difficult than to win an electoral victory. But it is also more rewarding.

Colette

*O*ut of the mouths of
babes and sucklings hast
thou ordained strength.

Psalms 8:2

*T*he world has no such
   flower in any land,
And no such pearl in any
   gulf the sea,
As any babe on any mother's
   knee.

Swinburne

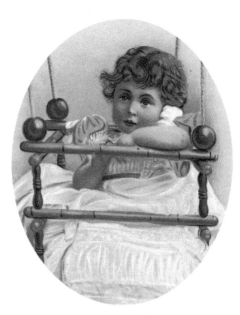

*I*s it hard to imagine what your family will be like with a new baby there? Just as you can have plenty of love for both your mom and dad, they can have plenty of love for both you *and* the new baby.

Mr. Rogers

*A*nd shall not loveliness
be loved forever?

Euripedes

*A*n ugly baby is a very nasty object—and the prettiest is frightful when undressed—till about four months; in short as long as they have their big body and little limbs and that terrible frog-like action.

Queen Victoria

*M*ankind owes to the
child the best it has to give.

U. N. Declaration

There are one hundred
and fifty-two distinctly different ways of holding a
baby—and all are right.

Heywood Broun

*B*y the time the youngest children have learned to keep the house tidy, the oldest grandchildren are on hand to tear it to pieces.

Christopher Morley

*H*OPE: You will figure it all out. And the best part is, you *enjoy* figuring it out. I mean, not all the time. But there's this moment when your baby cries and you pick her up and suddenly she's all smiles and making these sounds and—it's like magic.

thirtysomething

*S*leep, baby, sleep!
Thy father's watching the
   sheep,
Thy mother's shaking the
   dreamland tree,
And down drops a little
   dream for thee.
   Sleep, baby, sleep.

Elizabeth Prentiss